D0522638

THEORIES AND APPARITIONS

THEORIES AND APPARITIONS

Mark Doty

CAPE POETRY

Published by Jonathan Cape 2008

2 4 6 8 10 9 7 5 3 1

First published in Great Britain in 2008 by
Jonathan Cape
Random House, 20 Vauxhall Bridge Road,
London SW1V 2SA

www.rbooks.co.uk

Addresses for companies within The Random House Group Limited can be found
at: www.randomhouse.co.uk/offices.htm

The Random House Group Limited Reg. No. 954009

A CIP catalogue record for this book is available from the British Library

ISBN 9780224085281

The Random House Group Limited supports The Forest Stewardship
Council (FSC), the leading international forest certification organisation.
All our titles that are printed on Greenpeace approved FSC certified paper
carry the FSC logo. Our paper procurement policy can be found at:

CONTENTS

PIPISTRELLE

His music, Charles writes,
makes us avoidable.
I write: emissary of evening.

We're writing poems about last night's bat.
Charles has stripped the scene to lyric,
while I'm filling in the tale: how,

when we emerged from the inn,
an unassuming place in the countryside
near Hoarwithy, not far from the Wye,

two twilight mares in a thorn-hedged field
across the road – clotted cream
and raw gray wool, vaguely above it all –

came a little closer. Though
when we approached they ignored us
and went on softly tearing up audible mouthfuls,

so we turned in the other direction,
toward Lough Pool, a mudhole scattered with sticks
beneath an ancient conifer's vast trunk.

Then Charles saw the quick ambassador
fret the spaces between boughs
with an inky signature too fast to trace.

We turned our faces upward,
trying to read the deepening blue
between black limbs. And he said again,

There he is! Though it seemed only
one of us could see the fluttering pipistrelle
at a time – you'd turn your head to where

he'd been, no luck, he'd already joined
a larger dark. There he is! Paul said it,
then Pippa. Then I caught the fleeting contraption

speeding into a bank of leaves,
and heard the high, two-syllabled piping.
But when I said what I'd heard,

no one else had noticed it, and Charles said,
Only some people can hear their frequencies.
Fifty years old and I didn't know

I could hear the tender cry of a bat
– *cry* won't do: a diminutive chime
somewhere between merriment and weeping,

who could ever say? I with no music
to my name save what I can coax
into a line, no sense of pitch,

heard the night's own one-sided conversation.
What to make of the gift? An oddity,
like being double-jointed, or token

of some kinship to the little Victorian handbag
dashing between the dim bulks of trees?
Of course the next day we begin our poems.

Charles considers the pipistrelle's music navigational,
a modest, rational understanding of what
I have decided is my personal visitation.

Is it because I am an American I think the bat came
especially to address me, who have the particular gift
of hearing him? If he sang to us, but only I

heard him, does that mean he sang to me?
Or does that mean I am a son of Whitman,
while Charles is an heir of Wordsworth,

albeit thankfully a more concise one?
Is this material necessary or helpful to my poem,
even though Charles admires my welter

of detail, my branching questions?
Couldn't I compose a lean,
meditative evocation of what threaded

over our wondering heads,
or do I need to do what I am doing now,
and worry my little aerial friend

with a freight not precisely his?
Does the poem reside in experience
or in self-consciousness

about experience? Shh,
says the evening near the Wye.
Enough, say the hungry horses.

Listen to my poem, says Charles.
A word in your ear, says the night.

THE WORD

White cotton cap, immaculate shoes
and stockings, black coat over starched dress,
she performs her work, holds the book

open in front of her, looks down
through thick-rimmed glasses, glances up
swiftly so as not to lift her eyes long from the task,
covertly taking stock of who takes stock of her,

spine of the holy text in her left hand,
dark right forefinger tapping a random
or necessary passage, how has she chosen it?

I would say she beats out a jeremiad,
cannot or will not speak and so this iteration
is her form of witness – save that in her insistence
she strikes with the hard tap of her fingernail,

over and over, wearing the ink away until
the thin paper tears, lower half of the pages tatted,
as if mice had been shredding the blessings

and prohibitions for a nest, no choice
but to point to or punish the book or both,
tearing away at the damned loved word
that is everything to her and does not deliver her

and therefore she must go on wounding the book
in public: her art, displayed for us, unvarying,
in the station at 34th Street and Sixth Avenue,

on a bitter night just after the turn of the year.

IN THE AIRPORT MARSHES

A kind of heaven,
this clamor, a *lulliloo*:
'to shout joyously,
to welcome with cries,

from a cry of joy among
some African peoples':
Webster's New International,
1934, a foot-thick volume

deftly marbled
as this patch of marsh.
Today I require the term
and there it is – these definitions

wait to be lived,
actual as these frogs,
who chorus as if
there's no tomorrow,

or else they've all
the time in the world.
We ruin the rain,
they go right on,

this year. Hard to imagine
the eagerness of a body
which pours itself
into *this* – forms

you have to take on faith,
since all they seem
to be is chiming Morse
belling out long-short

over the patched tarmac
of the runway. I never till now
needed the word *lulliloo*.

How do you reckon your little music?

APPARITION (FAVORITE POEM)

The old words are dying,
everyone forgets them,
pages falling into sleep and dust,

dust and sleep, burning so slowly
you wouldn't even know there's a fire.
Or that's what I think half the time.

Then, at the bookstore, a young man reciting,
slight for fourteen, blond, without irony
but not self-important either;

his loping East Texas vowels threaten
to escape the fence of pentameter,
his voice seems to have just arrived here,

but the old cadence inhabits anyway.
He makes the poem his own
even as he becomes a vessel

for its reluctance to disappear.
All right, maybe they perish,
but the boy has the look of someone

repeating a crucial instruction
that must be delivered, word for word,
as he has learned it:

My name is Ozymandias, King of Kings,
Look on my Works, ye Mighty, and despair.

ANGEL OF PRAGUE

I have joined a student theatre group,
an insurrection in the motherly gray capital
battered by invasion and occupation

– exhausted somnolence, dreary romance.
In the piece we're mounting,
a demonstration in the central square,
I play the role of the Angel of Prague,

and must climb the façade of an ancient church
fronting the square, and stand behind the statue
of a female figure, a near-forgotten saint,

where I am to unfurl a pair of large fabric wings,
in my dream, my blue wing upon which is written,
IT MUST BE BEAUTIFUL, and my red wing
which reads IT MUST BE NEW.

I hold on to the waist of the statue
until I unfurl the second wing,
and then I must balance

on the narrow pedestal, or lean
against her stone back to support myself,
which is all right until I look down
the cold dizzying storeys to the pavement,

and gradually find myself furling
the cloth around her stone shoulders,
my legs trembling; it's hard to hold out

your arms when you're frightened
of being dashed on the stones below,

and in a while I slink down, back into the crowd,
where I shed my huge armature

and am praised for my performance
despite the fact that I feel defeated,
that I have given in to weakness

when I could, if I were stronger and less fearful,
I could have upheld those wings.

CITIZENS

The light turns and I'm stepping
onto the wide and empty crosswalk on Eighth Avenue,
nothing between the white lines but a blowing riffle

of paper when this truck –
all unnecessary red gleam – roars onto the avenue from 20th,
the driver turns his wheels inches from my knees

even though I jump back
out of the way, and before I've even thought I'm yelling
what are you doing, act like a citizen

though it's clear from the face
already blurred past me that he's enjoying this, and I'm yelling *Asshole*
and kick at the place where his tire was with my boot.

If I carried a sharp instrument
I could scrape a long howl on his flaming paint job
(just under the gold and looming logo: DEMOLITION)

and what kind of citizen
does this thought make me exactly, quivering and flummoxed
by contradictory impulses: to give a speech on empathy

or fling my double latte
across his back windshield, though who knows what
he might do then. He's stuck in traffic and pretends

I'm not watching him not looking
in my direction, and people passing doubtless think who is
this idiot fulminating to himself,

or probably they don't;
they've got trouble of their own. Here's a story:
two pilgrim monks arrive at a riverbank

where an old lady's weeping,
no way to cross, and though they've renounced
all traffic with women, one man hoists her on his shoulders

and ferries her over the water.
Later his friend is troubled: *How could you touch her
when you vowed not to?* And the first monk says, *I put her down*

on the other side of the river,
why are you still carrying her? Midday's so raw and dirty
I can't imagine anyone here's pleased by something just now,

and I'm carrying the devil
in his carbon chariot all the way to 23rd, down into the subway,
roiling against the impersonal malice of the truck that armors him

so he doesn't have to know anyone.
Under the Port Authority I understand I'm raging because
that's easier than weeping, which is what I want not because I'm so
     afraid

of scraping my skull
on the pavement but because he's made me erasable,
a slip of a self, subject to. How'd I get emptied

till I can be hostaged
by a dope in a flaming climate-wrecker? I try to think
who made him so powerless he craves dominion over strangers,

11

but you know what?
I don't care. If he's one of those people miserable for lack
of what is found in poetry, fine.

It's not him I'm sorry for.
It's every person on this train burrowing deeper uptown
as if it were screwing further down into the bedrock.

Heavy hands on the knees,
weary heads nodding toward the floor or settling
against the glass. When did I ever set anything down?

APPARITION

Chilly noon on Seventh,
and I swear in the window
of the Eros Diner, corner
of 21st Street,

John Berryman's eating alone,
back against the wall,
face tilted down toward
his meal, iconic thick glasses

glinting like the sidewalk
in the cold, iconic thick beard
nodding a little as he lifts
his spoon, intent

on lunch, so happy
that a plate's in front
of him he never bothers
to look up at me.

HOUSE OF BEAUTY

In Jersey City, on Tonnelle Avenue,
the House of Beauty is burning.

On a Sunday morning in January,
under the chilly shadow of the Pulaski Skyway,
the House of Beauty is burning.

Who lobbed the firebottle through the glass,
in among the crèmes and thrones,
the helmets and clippers and combs,
who set the House of Beauty burning?

In the dark recess beside the sink
– where heads lay back to be laved
under the perfected heads rowed along the walls –
the hopeful photographs of possibility darken,
now that the House of Beauty is burning.

The Skyway beetles in the ringing cold,
trestle arcing the steel river and warehouses,
truck lots and Indian groceries,
a new plume of smoke joining the others,
billow of dark thought rising
from the broken forehead of the House of Beauty

– an emission almost too small to notice, just now,
alarm still ringing, the flames new-launched
on their project of ruining an effort at pleasure,
glass jutting like cracked ice in the window frame,
no one inside, the fire department on the way.
All things by nature, wrote Virgil, *are ready to get worse*;
no surprise, then, that the House of Beauty is burning.

Though whatever happens, however far
these fires proceed, reducing history to powder,
whatever the House of Beauty made is untouchable now;
nothing can undo so many heads made lovely
or at least acceptable, so much shapelessness
given what are called permanents, though nothing holds
a fixed form. Bring on the flames,
what does it matter if the house is burning?

Propose a new beauty, perennially unhoused:
neither the lost things nor the fire itself,
but the objects in their dresses of disaster,
anything clothed in its own passage:
padded vinyl chair burst into smoky tongues,
Lucite helmet sagged to a new version of its dome.
Our black bridge, a charred rainbow on iron legs,
two ruby eyes glowering from its crown.
If beauty *is* burning, what could you save?
The house of beauty is a house of flames.

THEORY OF THE SOUL

Ligustrum, penicillium
three ragweeds, fusarium, marshelder, pollen of timothy, sweet vernal,
cocklebur and feathers, dog and tuna, dust mite, milk and yolk:

the allergist's assistant
pierces the skin of my back with ten clusters of needles,
each dipped in tinctures, and we wait to see which ones make me
    sick.

She says, You're okay, right?
and leaves the room. I'm a little tired, holding my face
in my hands, warm, leaning forward,

and then a doctor says,
How long ago did you give him that shot? A nurse says, Ten minutes.
A shot? Adrenaline, the doctor says, you had an allergic reaction

to the allergy test.
I thought if you blacked out you'd see it like a movie,
people gathering above your head, but of course I wasn't there

to know I was gone.
Later, when I tell Claudia, she says, How can you know when you're
    not awake?
Ten minutes, no perception – just a little queasy,

then a jump cut
and I'm the hot center of a buzzing host afraid I'll sue them
because they've injected me with solutions of mouse hair, lobster and
    egg,

and left me to my own devices.
I tell Claudia this is what troubles me: I've been around enough dying
to trust that last breath wings out something more than air –

But where was I,
or that, if the self's embalmed by an injection of seafood and dust?
Animation, intelligence, the gathered weight of half a century

switched off like a lamp?
And then I tell her – well, Claudia isn't even in the room,
I'm talking to the Claudia I carry around in my head,

as we address our friends
in solitary moments, driving or walking uptown to the market –
I don't know why I tell her about the black kid

in the dingy passageway
to the L yesterday singing early Beatles with a radical purity,
everything distilled to a bright arcing liquid vulnerability

spilling over,
and the amaryllis bulbs in the florist's window flinging their bodies
forward in order to arrive at red, the single term of their arrival –

self made visible
in the reach for a form, breath in this body then
that, passed on or gone, and maybe that's why

we love to kiss,
because then we come closest to the exhaled quick.
We are what we make? Yeah, Claudia says,

all that. But where
is my work, while I'm prone on the allergist's floor?
The doctor who recommends, once I am breathing regularly,

that I avoid oysters,
and encourages me to call him again.

APPARITION

Handsome chest thick with white hair cropped close,
the pleasant man leans the stacked solid volume

of himself back to rest, reclining on his pillows, and I sit back
on my knees to take stock of him, but the look

sucks the breath out of me: he is gazing in my direction
with a pleased half smile, eyes a little out of focus, as though I'm
    seeing him

or he views me through a kind of gauze, and he isn't the man I
    know – slightly –
but, plain as early winter daylight

across the Hudson, the impossible gentle manly visionary
of the eighteen-fifties, bowl-cut hair, warm lines around the eyes

dilated as by an opiate, what shines in
and out of them in equal proportion –

That's the Walt Whitman who has come to look at me,
curiously, on a mild November afternoon on the west side of
    Midtown.

THEORY OF BEAUTY (TONY)

Somebody who worked in the jailhouse kitchen
cooked up some grease, burnt it black, scraped
the carbon from the griddle. Somebody made a needle
from the shaft of a filched Bic, ballpoint replaced

with a staple beaten flat; then the men received,
one at a time, faces of Christ looking up through
streams of blood from a thorny crown,
or death's heads looming over x's of bones.

But Tony chose, for his left shoulder, a sign language
glyph, a simple shape, though hard to read;
he had to tell me what it meant. He flicked
his lighter and spilled flecks of dope on the towel

across his lap, brushed his bare stomach as though
he might have set himself aflame. He said,
It stands for Love. Then what seemed indifferently
drawn, hardly a sketch, became a blazon

that both lifted and exposed the man who wore it,
as he fumbled with the lighter, too stoned to fire
the pipe he held, using it to point to the character
on his arm, making plain the art of what was written there.

THEORY OF BEAUTY
(GREENWICH AVENUE)

Thirty-seven clocks in five tiers.

Mantel, cuckoo,
rusticated, ormolu, glass-domed, moving brass balls and chimes,
porcelain, bronze-figured French:
thirty-seven, ranged in the shop window,
not especially attractive,

none fine, none precious,
even to my taste individually desirable.
But studying them, then turning away

into the end of a mild afternoon
the hand of winter's never quite let go of,

warmly tinted but almost heatless sunlight,
buildings ahead in silhouette, and then
the urge to turn back to the stepped rows

and suddenly the preeminently important thing
is their fulfillment of the category *clock*,

the divergence of means
of occupying that name, honoring the terms
and intent of it but nonetheless

presenting a various set of faces
to the avenue, in the warm light
of the shop. Then I or you, whoever's

doing the looking, understands
that this is the city's particular signature,

the range of possibilities within any single set,
and what is pleasing is not the individual clock

(goofy or kitsch, in their frostings and columns,
scrollworks and gildings) but the degree

to which it belongs and at the same time
pushes towards the edges of difference –

so the window's
thirty-seven branching aspects

of a single notion,
almost absurd in their essentially useless variety.
And when you turn away again,

there on the sidewalk
is a perfect instance of the category *sink*,

in this case *kitchen*,
singular instance of all its category
in the five boroughs,

a double stainless model
battered around the drain, humbled at its edges,

rim a little crumpled, but the interior
shining from a lifetime of scouring,

and beauty resides not within
individual objects but in the nearly
unimaginable richness of their relation.

THEORY OF MULTIPLICITY

I don't like the laundromat on 16th Street in the winter,
the single aisle between washers and dryers too narrow
to allow one to sit down, and the women who work there
doing the laundry of others seem to resent one's in-the-wayness,
and why aren't you paying them to do your wash anyway?

But in summer it's fine: you can read on the street, in plastic chairs
set out for this purpose, watch people go by, and, as I liked to do
one September, look into the garden someone made next door
on the edge of the sidewalk, spilling onto the pavement,
surprisingly wild, with prairie grasses, a shrubby coneflower,
strapping and blowsy black-eyed Susan, even a few bees

frowsing through it – how do they live, in Manhattan?
Leaning back on the legs of the white chair, staring into the green,
I thought of myself as one of its many viewers. What I knew
was this singular aspect, this vantage, in this light,
but didn't its actuality consist in being seen multiply?

Those who did not ignore it in their hurry took it in
from the particular height or angle afforded them,
and even those who paid no mind must have registered,
subtly, the tumbled blur of periphery. What was
the garden but the sum of all that, studied or casual?
Perception carried, loved, considered, dis- or regarded,

late in the season, frost probably not far off, afternoon
slanting down from the London plane trees, already yellowed
and thinning leaves, sunlight humming into the stalks
and flowers, the garden I saw one occasion of many,
and this was in some way an accomplishment,

a contribution to the work; it took all of us to make
the garden known. No one could assemble
the entire vantage we made together,
if anyone could . . . I felt in that moment
not dissolved in anything, not selfless, but joined
in a layering of singularities – a multiplicity

not God, exactly, that theoretical viewpoint,
but a satisfying gesture in that direction.
The next summer the garden would be sparse,
not well tended, and offer no consolation,
though even its diminishment might be said
to be one of its nearly endless dimensions.

THEORY OF BEAUTY
(GRACKLES ON MONTROSE)

Eight o'clock, warm Houston night,
and in the parking lot the grackles
hold forth royally, in thick trees

on the lip of traffic, and either
they're oblivious to the street-rush
and come-and-go at the Kroger

or else they actually like it, our hurry
a useful counter to their tintinnabulation.
Now one's doing the Really Creaky Hinge,

making it last a long time;
now Drop the Tin Can, glissando,
then Limping Siren, then it's back

to the Hinge done with a caesura
midstream, so it becomes a Recalcitrant Double Entry.
What are they up to, these late, randy singers,

who seem to shiver the whole tree in pleasure
when somebody gets off a really fierce line,
pirate aerial deejays remixing their sonics

above the median strip all up and down
the block from here to the Taco Cabana?
They sample Bad Brakes, they do

Tea Kettle in Hell, Slidewhistle
into Car Alarm, Firecracker with a Bright Report,
and every feathered body –

how many of them *are* there,

obscured by dense green?
seems to cackle over that one,
incendiary rippling, pure delight,

imperious, impure singing:
traffic in tongues, polyglot,
expansive, awry.

THEORY OF BEAUTY (POMPEII)

Tiny girl in line at the café — seven, eight? — holding her book open,
pointing to the words and saying them half-aloud
while her mother attends to ordering breakfast;

she's reading POMPEII . . . *Buried Alive!* with evident delight.
Pleasure with a little shiver inside it.

And that evening, I thought I was no longer afraid
of the death's head beneath the face of the man beneath me.

THEORY OF MARRIAGE

I have a slight thrumming aura of backache,
so Marie — we've met for a late lunch before a movie,
at a Greek place in the West Village — says

What you need is the chi gong parlor,
so we take a cab to a vague block between SoHo and Chinatown
— Marie has to look to find it — and once she's spotted

the flight of scarlet stairs leading down from the street,
she leaves us at the door, benevolently, as if to say,
Here, my dears, is the gift I've led you to.

We're ushered into a long room
bright as a nail salon,
various citizens, entirely dressed

but for coat and shoes, prone upon many tables,
as we are, in a moment, Paul an aisle away from me.

His masseur's an intense, strapping man;
mine an intense, compact woman
who asks what sort of treatment I require
and soon pushes against various points
along my spine, knots of tension loosening, and soon I'm fading

under the specific presence of touch; no more bright chamber
full of sore New Yorkers, no more street noise, shoppers,

no more various and polyphonic expressions
of desire, no desire really, just press and release

here and here, awareness moving
from one instance to the next.

Is that the cure, for subjectivity
to diminish to a singular point of attention,
everything but this floated away?

All too soon it's over, and the masseuse says,

Your friend not done, you want do more?
Sure, I say. *Feet*, she says? Almost before I've nodded we're off,
the pushing exploring regions that do not seem

to exist until pressed. And then the self's
a glass fishbowl dropped from some great height,
falling slowly, at ease, shattering

without a sound,

and just as the weightless fish go fantailing free,
I'm aware that Paul is crying, *Ow!*

and then I hear his masseur say, *Your friend not done,*
you want more? And he must think he may as well,
since I am still releasing the contained sounds of one

pushed into new life, until my treatment

comes to an end and the woman says,
Friend not done, we do head?
And as a resistance I didn't know

was there is banished,
I am dimly aware that the masseur
has climbed onto Paul's back, Paul is crying *Oh, ow!*

And just as I am vanishing again into the heaven
of rubbed temples, where no city exists except the one

in which the skull produces a repetitive, golden music,
somewhere far away Paul's masseur says, *your friend* . . .

In this way we spend a small but substantive fortune,

a sum which would have been even greater
had I not cried out, as my masseuse left my hands and wrists
and prepared to commence elsewhere,

Stop, enough, no! To Paul's huge relief,
since he thought I must want to continue,
and therefore he must persist while I am persisting,
even though he was in pain, strong-armed by his assailant,

and I thought he wanted to go on and therefore
I must endure the bliss that had become an exhaustion,

and we walked out onto the street relieved,
late for the movies, Paul limping a little,
my backache gone.

THEORY OF MARRIAGE
(THE HUG)

Arden would turn his head toward the one
he loved, Paul or me, and look downward,
and butt the top of his skull against us, leaning forward,
hiding his face, disappearing into what he'd chosen.

Beau had another idea. He'd offer his rump
for scratching, and wag his tail while he was stroked,
returning that affection by facing away, looking out
toward whatever might come along to enjoy.

Beau had no interest in an economy of affection;
why hoard what you can give away?
Arden thought you should close your eyes
to anything else; only by vanishing

into the beloved do you make it clear:
what else is there you'd want to see?

THEORY OF NARRATIVE

Oh, you're a writer, I'm a writer, too, Juan says,
I write novels, I've written eight of them, I'll tell you one.

The sun isn't even up, Juan's driving
our taxi in the high desert north of Mexico City,
I've had no coffee, two hours to the airport in Leon,
chill air astringent with mesquite smoke and diesel fumes,
there is no coffee in all the world.

This guy, he wants to be a musician, see?
His grandfather encourages him, but his father says,
you must be a doctor, so he goes to medical school,
he studies for years, but there's a revolution,
the clinic's shut down, and he comes home
and finds a hidden note that says,
Dig under the peach tree.
So he gets a shovel and starts digging, everybody comes out
and says what are you doing, are you crazy, there's a revolution,
but he keeps digging, and wrapped in the roots
there's a wooden box, roots are clinging to the box, right?
But he opens the lid, and lifts out a violin,
an instrument his grandfather hid for him,
and when he starts to play it the air fills with the scent of peaches.

This is the beginning of the first story,
a political drama involving the healing powers of the violin,
which lead, after many developments, to the death of Stalin,
and then to the second novel,

a moral fable involving a snake
who swallows a conniving prune,
so that the fruit can sprout in the earth and become a tree.

Early in this tale I realize Juan will not stop,
not for a moment, and Paul is pretending to sleep in the backseat
so that I seem to be alone with Juan,
and have no other role than assent,

expected to respond at each inquiry – see? right? –
to indicate that I have not ceased to pay the fare
of my attention. Only so much can be done
with the tale of the foolish serpent and wise prune,

out the window the unchartable desert
slowly lightening . . . You know? asks Juan,

and suddenly I don't. What am I assenting to,
I am shrinking as each detail is placed into its context,
mmm, uh-huh . . . Has Juan written these stories
at all, is making them up as he drives into
the slow dawning, are we even going toward Leon?

Now he will try another direction,
and without transition begins the tale
of a woman observed by a frightening voyeur
who sees her every move as she undresses,

and who in the end is revealed – all my stories, Juan says,
are ironical – to be a mosquito,
which she swats, but not before the tiny beast
has infected her with West Nile virus.

A turn that seems to lead down an even darker path
since the next novel's a grotesque family tale
concerning two brothers, one bound in a wheelchair,
and how they plot to poison their vile old father.
But instead of eating the cookies they have prepared for him,

the old guy feeds the arsenical pastries to their own children,
and is even now enjoying his sons' wives, as he writes
in a farewell letter composed in disappearing ink,

because he has committed
the perfect crime, which is this:
I can't get out, have to hear
what happens next, the *further*
of the tires melded to the forwardness of plot.

Is Juan an artist possessed by his work, or a maniac
who wields power through endless, implacable narration?
I cannot look at the great lyric desert
under the new sun because I am hostaged by causality
and chronology, afraid of being put out

in the ditch beside the road,
since the storyteller holds all the power,
and I will not be released
until each character is dead
or meted out an ironical fate,

I am a nodding yes
to a prepossessing will, and is there
an airport anywhere ahead of us,
is there a Leon at all? I can tell you nothing
of the remaining novels. I am party to them,
weakly, as we hurtle past the smolder

of extinguished grass fires,
citizens awaiting a bus in the cold,
men gathering at an open-air café winking awake
under a string of bulbs hung between wooden posts,
the bodies of dogs struck and lying on the roadside.

(I think Juan himself might have killed them,
driving and driving in the night, telling his endless tales.)

I never want to tell another story, or be told one.
Let the fragments hang in beautiful suspension,
let incident and detail float without ever linking,
I want to be quiet between little ribbons of speech,

the tyranny of connection
erases the lateral, chains us
to the future, endlessly woven lines
of action I could not begin, now, to remember,
since narrative had gotten what it wanted:

I wasn't there to receive the tale.

Of course we arrived
in mid-story, and Juan pulled over
to the curb and continued to talk,
as if to see how long I would remain listening
while the eighth of his tales wound on,

and when we staggered out of the cab,
hoisting luggage up onto the airport curb,

I was too sick to even feel relieved,
and Paul, gone a pale, peculiar shade
like blanched celery – I do not exaggerate,
although I have, for the sake of a good story –
bent over and vomited onto the sidewalk.

As though we had narrative poisoning,
made to swallow our own medicine
until we choked on it, held too long
to an enlarging mirror
aswarm with vengeful fathers and conniving fruit,
gullible snakes and Orphic musicians,

and even, somewhere, the stuff
of the four other novels which simply refused to register
in my memory.
                    – Oh, one more: a man returns
to his old home town,
his grandfather's written him a letter to introduce him
to the spirit of the place,

he's reading only a bit at a time,
on a bench in the public square,
of course he's reading,
moved from moment to moment by
the implacable agency of a narrator,

though the message is half-understood,
never delivered, received partially or late –

so he doesn't understand till the last paragraph
he's already dead, which is why his grandfather says
don't be afraid of the butterflies,

and through a pulsing wall of wings he goes – see? –
into the other side.

APPARITION

Oracular pear,

this peacock
perched in a plywood roost
at the garden center,

magnificent behind a wire fence
marked with his name:
Hommer

(pronounced
without the extra m),
and hand-lettered instructions:

DON'T PROVOKE ME.

He's the provocation:
of what use
the wrought extravagance

he's not just now displaying?
Darwin: 'The sight of a feather
in a peacock's tail,

whenever I gaze at it,
makes me sick!'
No reason on earth

even eons of increments

would conspire to this,
and is the peahen
that hard to attract,

requiring an arc of nervous gleams,
a hundred shining animals
symmetrically peering

from the dim
primeval woods?
But if Hommer argues

by his mere presence

for creation, his deity's
a little hysteric,
rampant attitude

contained in all that glory.
Did he who made the lamb
make this imperious

metallic topknot shivering
above an emerald field
of anodized aluminum

while Hommer blinks and flicks

his actual eyes from side to side?
And then the epic
trombone-slide-from-Mars cry

no human throat can mime
– is that why it stops the heart? –
just before he condescends to unfurl

the archaic poem of his tail.

THEORY OF THE SUBLIME

You will, said Carlos, be in my project?

Carlos is a painter who no longer makes use of paint;
his finished work will be a room of monitors,
on each screen a different person clapping;

I am simply to sit and clap my hands together
while Carlos videotapes, for as long as I like.

Beginning's a little awkward,
self-conscious, even though the camera's set on a tripod
and Carlos is hiding his considerable beauty behind a large chair;

I'm reaching for some sort of rhythm to perform,
turning my attention away from the afternoon
sunlight in the tall windows of the studio

– but then what simply begins to take place,
a minute into the voyage, *is* a rhythm,
a pattern arising from – the body? –

and the pulse becomes firmer, more persistent,
life of a tree unfurling, green burl spreading out
its swath of selfhood, an actuality:

the clapping is a night-crowd of leaves
billowing out to obscure the quick chips of stars.
The soul occupies the night-town,

reclining in the shadowy chairs, the soil
looms darkly beneath, soul spurts up out of there,
chard raising its green ribs up over a black field

– all signaled, clapped out in the hurry
of one hand sharp against another

rising further until it's alternately praise and outrage,

praise for the world
held against the inevitable
fierce accusation any singularity is,
any lifting individual arc,

that spiraling like climbing the steep winding
of the cathedral in Barcelona, the Sagrada Familia,
stone steps built to the mathematics of a narrow seashell,

feet obscured in darkness, a built night,
and then in a while, many whorls up,
the terrifying small balconies

perched at the back of spires of conch
or chestnut burr or whatever spiked and tiled intensity
the architect pronged from his melting fantasia,

his program of severe transformation,

his enforced (well, no one made me go there,
but once you start up there is no backing out)
passageways into the sublime.

Further, after the little resting platforms,
to strange arched bridges flung between
towering honeycombs,

an unfurled vegetal perch
behind a glazed cypress studded with thick white doves,
up into pinnacles of smashed golden tile,

wounds encrusted in glass, extrusions
of fruit and stone gathering like wax
at the lip of a candle,

I'm mounting a vast beeswax taper,
a honeycombed thing thrusting unlikely,

perfectly solid and somehow entirely unstable.
Far out there is the Mediterranean, tip of a crane,
barking, a dog run down in the square,

sharp green parrots like flying jewels
tussling over scraps of rolls,
and then, at the height of my clapping,
when I can push no further into the thinning air,

perched at a ridiculous and frail slip of masonry
holding together or apart two enameled narwhal tusks
aimed at the next, at the forwardness,

at the limit of praise, when flesh

begins to reassert that it is welded
to the giddy soul trying to get out from the top of the head,

body that's climbed all the way to the tip
of the concrete vertebra
and now contemplates stepping off,

a few tourists snapping photographs as if to hold at bay
the tremendous incipient vertigo and ambition of it.

Then begins the winding
down the towers again,
down swifter than up, light-headed,

body in darkness, flush with the crazy excelsis
of the tower, raked, out of breath, a little sick with all that glory,
stumbling a bit, hands stinging on the railing,

coming to rest, like a pigeon from a long high flight,
as if to land too swiftly and cease the motion of wings
would somehow injure the heart,

so one must land carefully, making out of bare soil
a little container by pressing one's own breast
and belly into the earth,

and when I come to a complete stop the silence
seems extraordinarily firm and authoritative,

and Carlos rises up from behind the tall chair
where he's been hiding to nod his head approvingly,
to indicate that something has happened here,

and in a while I ask how long I've been clapping,
shaking out my stinging hands,

and Carlos looks at his watch and says, Thirty-six minutes,
the room crackling with accusation or prayer.

To what thrills and defeats us: defiance and applause.

TO JOAN MITCHELL

At twilight the locusts begin,
waves and waves,
nothing to do with lamentation.

No one's told them the world is ending;
they proceed as always,
everything subsumed into –

you can't call it a cry, exactly, no singularity in it,
but the thousands, the ten thousand
– voices?

★

       Not singing.
Audible undulation, the waves
these bodies make. Seamless, encompassing,
filling Branard Street –

★

As it should be.
I want them not knowing,
in this way the sound becomes a kind of refuge,

filled with safety and splendor.

★

Or it's more like the big sound
puts its hands under your arms and elevates you,
effortless,
gyrating momentum pulls one upward with it,
collective ululation
having become a unified rising motion

      like her great canvas,
in four panels,
continuous field so charged
as to fill the room in which it hangs
with an inaudible humming,

as if to erase the gallery over which it triumphs.

Almost audible:

weft of continuous color, blocks of mint,
      green-yellow glaze, olive

floating above a violet
      underpainting, contentious

against the citron and yellow-flung,
      seamless texture,

      like the *hare* of the cicadas,
ceaseless music through which outbreaks of blue

assert themselves.
As if she'd made the human equivalent
      of their spiralling, and this was faith.

★

No trust ever held
      in constancy

— only what's relinquished
      over and over

has about it the heft
of the genuine –

The canvas firmly centered in its living,
drenched, upright
posture of its color –

the authority of her green

more firmly itself than anyone in the room –
★

In the flashpoint summer of 2002
it was possible to feel where we were headed,

sun screwing its titanium compress down
on human foreheads in the parking lots,

thin tamarisks on the margin shimmering a little
as if seen through fumes of gasoline,

and I was in the absolute darkness of Fresno,
past the middle of my life. As if I'd been colonized

by the long swathes of car lots, flapping pennants
stunned under the mercury lamps,

will and inwardness thinned
like the chemical haze over the lettuce fields,

smokes risen from torn-up vineyards,
weary vines heaped for burning . . .

Then a guy in a leather bar – wisdom itself
I swear in an ordinary, bearded face –

held my right hand and stared down
into the contradictory fretwork, drawn

to me and not going home with me,
nothing as simple as that,

though we were two spiked intensities
of pulse and aura, he was holding back

an enormous force of perception,
translating the lines in my palm, and he said

to me the one possible thing I'd believe:
Sometimes you just have to make

a little faith. That fountaining canvas,
expanse of presence in the museum room,

organized and intensified vitality,
ineradicable in spite of the new void we've made

looming everywhere over the vineyards
and shopping centers and car lots from here

to Houston to New York City, relentless, locked in,
poised to erase. The picture spoke its green.

MAGIC MOUSE

Scrap of fur or fabric scrambles hand to hairy wrist,
flees into the hole thumb and forefinger make
in the fist, most warm days, Sixth Avenue and 14th Street:

big-headed guy squats hands outstretched and the toy
slips knuckle to back of the other hand, scurries to the nest
as if of its own volition while he blares over and over

same flat vowels, somehow half the time trumping
layered horns and airbrakes and din of no apparent origin,
raising his terms above the avenue as if he peddled

not the thing itself but its unprintable name:
MAHJIK MAOWWZ,
his accomplishment, a phrase the alphabet refuses.

MAH as in *Nah* as in *No way, JIK* the voice's arc
fallen hard back to the sidewalk, *MAOWWZZ*
a bridge with a long slide in the center. It won't work

unless you're loud, seal your nasal passages,
inflect five syllables in blat and euphony,
then the little three-syllable follow-through,

price-tag vocalise tailing away like an afterthought:
ONE DOLLAH. Even halfway down the block he's altered
the air, made the spine around which some fraction

of city arranges itself, his beautiful thing
in diminishing coda as you're further away:
Magic Mouse, one dahlah. I practice, I can't

get it right. Maybe what's required is resistance:

indifferent citizens impelled in four directions,
scraps of cell-phone recitations into private ethers,

mechanical sobs his syllables cut through and against.
Maybe it's the sheer persistence of the ugly span
of phrase lifting up and over what it's built to represent.

Or else the engine of his song's the nothing
that could contain that tumbling scrappy model
of a living thing in his hands,

so he says it again and again

– while the little toy, all the word
won't hold, always escaping,
goes on with its astonishing work.

APPARITION

Bitter wind off a metal harbor
and here's Alan Dugan crossing 15th Street
as if he owns it, sharp new jacket
just the shade of that riffled steel

– why shouldn't the dead sport
a little style?
        Once, at a dinner
in his honor, I watched bored Dugan
take out a pair of clippers and begin to trim
his nails, till a fat yellow paring flew
and landed on the plate of his publisher's wife,
who screamed. Then the recalcitrant old boho
grew courtly, and, with a smile that may
have been sincere, managed to convince her

he was a gentleman after all.
And here he is in the afterlife,
big glasses gleaming, standing up straight
as he never could in the years I knew him,
no chip on *his* shoulder

– you can tell by the shiny jacket
he's over all that now.

THEORY OF INCOMPLETION

I'm painting the apartment, elaborate project,
edging doorways and bookcases,

two coats at least, and on the radio
– the cable opera station – something
I don't know, Handel's *Semele*,

and either it's the latex fumes or the music itself
but I seem never to have heard anything so radiant,

gorgeous rising tiers of it
ceasing briefly then cascading again,
as if baroque music were a series of waterfalls

pouring in the wrong direction, perpetually up
and up, twisting toward the empyrean.

When a tenor – playing the role of a god,
perhaps the god of art? – calls for unbridled joy
the golden form of his outburst

matches the solar confidence of its content,
and I involuntarily say, *ah*,

I am so swept up by the splendor,
on my ladder, edging the trim
along the crown molding, up where

the fumes concentrate. I am stroking
the paint onto every formerly white inch,
and of course I know *Semele* will end,

but it doesn't seem it ever has to:
this seemingly endless chain of glorious conclusions,

writhing stacked superb filigree
– let it open out endlessly,
let door after door be slid back

to reveal the next cadence,
the new phrasing, onward and on.

I am stilled now, atop my ladder,
leaning back onto the rungs, am the rapture
of denied closure, no need to go anywhere,

entirety forming and reasserting itself, an endless
– self-enfolding, self-devouring –

of which Handel constructs a model
in music's intricate apportionment
of minutes. And then there's barely a beat

of a pause before we move on to Haydn,
and I am nowhere near the end of my work.

ACKNOWLEDGEMENTS

Acknowledgements are due to the editors of the following:

Alaska Quarterly, American Poetry Review, Bayou, Bloom, Ecotone, Five Points, Harvard Divinity Bulletin, London Review of Books, Lumina, Magma, McSweeney's, Ploughshares, Prairie Schooner, Runes, TriQuarterly, Water-Stone Review